MW00883813

My Basketball Journal

This Journal Belongs to:

_____

HOW TO USE THIS JOURNAL

This journal will give you a step by step guide to make sure you are improving your basketballs skills everyday. This journal has the power to help you chart both your mental and physical pursuits to improve.

The start of this journal will provide an explanation of how and why to record different skills and goals. The book will then provide sample workouts and exercises. The bulk of the book will provide a daily template to chart your daily workouts, goals, and reflections.

Research shows that to effectively accomplish goals is to break large goals down into daily goals. To accomplish daily goals it is essential to create routines that provide the necessary time and attention to be your best. The simple tool of writing down your goals and tracking them daily is immensely helpful in becoming the person and player you desire to be.

CONTENTS

ACKNOWLEDGMENTS

I'd like to thank my love G, my parents, and my dear friend Melo. I'd further like to acknowledge Tim Ferriss, Brian Johnson, Tony Robbins, and the many other leaders teaching how we can best optimize our lives. I want to extend immense gratitude to Steve Fisher and the San Diego State Men's Basketball coaching staff in helping teach me the game.

- Step back, side step jumpers off dribble
- Pull up jumpers off a dribble move
- Catch and shoot 3 pt range
- Catch at 3 point line and attack: pull up jumper around free throw line off one or two dribbles
- Confidently attack dribble: In and Out Dribble, Crossover, Behind the Back, Through the Legs and Spin Move
- Reverse layups
- Off hand layups
- Euro step, floater, or pro hop layups
- Shoot off 1 bounce
- Jab step/Pump Fake to get to shot or layup
- Make strong dribble move to get to a shot or layup
- Free throw range shooting
- Jump stop layup
- Dribble to layup off 1 foot
- Balanced shooting with followthrough in the key
- Dribble fullcourt with head up
- Dominant hand layups

Above is an example of a Hierarchy of Skills Chart. This would likely be used for an elementary or middle school student. With the bottom of the chart the skills you want to master before you move up. Once you master the skill you want to move up the list to add more skills to your game. You want to make sure that you continue to practice the skills at the bottom but find different drills to increase the difficulty of performing the skill.

Complete your own Hierarchy of Skills Chart.
What would you like to work on the most? The
harder skills are on top and the fundamental skills
will be written on the bottom.

You can write on the lines or all around the
pyramid to best illustrate what skills your are
looking to work on.

Gratitude

Why is it important to write down daily what you are thankful for?

On each daily journal page there is a portion of the page asking you to write 2 things you are thankful for. Scientists and psychologists agree that when we focus on what is going positive in our life it will lead to greater happiness and the ability to withstand difficult changes or unexpected circumstances. When you write your two answers they can be both large ideas or the smallest details of what you are thankful for.

Example:
I am thankful for:

1.   this gentle breeze through the window
2.   my body being able to move and play ball

Goal Setting

Why and how to set goals?

Goal setting is crucial to accomplishing your pursuits. If you don't know what your goals are it is nearly impossible to live the life you want. You are also far more likely to accomplish your goals if you write them down and make it a habit of reviewing your goals daily, weekly, monthly, and yearly.

In order to accomplish big goals you must break down your goals in smaller chunks. For example if you wanted to become a more accurate 3 point shooter you goal setting might look something like below.

3 Month Goal: Increase my 3 point accuracy by making 3,000 three pointers this Summer.

Month Goal: Make 1,000 three pointers in game like drills during workouts.

Weekly Goals: Make 250 three pointers a week.

Daily Goal: Make 50 three pointers each weekday (Make 10 in the left corner, 10 in the left wing, 10 top of the key, 10 in the right wing, 10 in the right corner).

Monthly Goals

Month _____

_____
_____
_____
_____
_____

Month _____

_____
_____
_____
_____
_____

Month _____

_____
_____
_____
_____
_____

Weekly Goals

Week 1: Date _____

Week 2: Date _____

Week 3: Date _____

Week 4: Date _____

Week 5: Date _____

Week 6: Date _____

Week 7 : Date _____

Week 8 : Date _____

Week 9 : Date _____

Game Log

The next 8 pages have space for keeping track of your performance in games. This can be for official games, practice scrimmages, or pickup games at your local gym or outdoor court. The point is to track what you do well and what you need to improve on so you know what to focus your training and skill development on. The last questions asks you to evaluate your performance as a teammate. It's important to remember no matter how talented you are individually your ability to work within a team is crucial to becoming the best player you can be.

Game Log

Date: _____

Played Against: _____

Location _____

Notes on the Game:

_____

_____

_____

_____

_____

_____

_____

_____

_____

What I did best:

_____

What I can improve or what I learned:

_____

Was I a good teammate? Yes/No? Explain

_____

Game Log

Date: _____

Played Against: _____

Location _____

Notes on the Game:

_____

_____

_____

_____

_____

_____

_____

_____

_____

What I did best:

_____

What I can improve or what I learned:

_____

Was I a good teammate? Yes/No? Explain

_____

Game Log

Date: _____

Played Against: _____

Location _____

Notes on the Game:

_____

_____

_____

_____

_____

_____

_____

_____

_____

What I did best:

_____

What I can improve or what I learned:

_____

Was I a good teammate? Yes/No? Explain

_____

Game Log

Date: _____

Played Against: _____

Location _____

Notes on the Game:

_____

_____

_____

_____

_____

_____

_____

_____

_____

What I did best:

_____

What I can improve or what I learned:

_____

Was I a good teammate? Yes/No? Explain

_____

Game Log

Date: _____

Played Against: _____

Location _____

Notes on the Game:

_____

_____

_____

_____

_____

_____

_____

_____

_____

What I did best:

_____

What I can improve or what I learned:

_____

Was I a good teammate? Yes/No? Explain

_____

Game Log

Date: _____
Played Against: _____
Location _____

Notes on the Game:

_____
_____
_____
_____
_____
_____
_____
_____
_____
_____

What I did best:

What I can improve or what I learned:

Was I a good teammate? Yes/No? Explain

Game Log

Date: _____
Played Against: _____
Location _____

Notes on the Game:

_____
_____
_____
_____
_____
_____
_____
_____
_____

What I did best:

_____

What I can improve or what I learned:

_____

Was I a good teammate? Yes/No? Explain

_____

Game Log

Date: _____
Played Against: _____
Location _____

Notes on the Game:

_____
_____
_____
_____
_____
_____
_____
_____
_____
_____

What I did best:

_____

What I can improve or what I learned:

_____

Was I a good teammate? Yes/No? Explain

_____

Create your own Workout

With todays technology the access to free useful content has never been easier. There really shouldn't be any excuses if you want to get better. Resources through books, articles, the internet, social media, and especially YouTube make it easier than ever to find helpful drills to improve your skills.

When researching drills it is important to consult a coach or someone you know is knowledgeable about basketball. Some helpful hints: you can even search your favorite players, NBA teams, or college teams and find information on what drills their trainers are practicing with their players.

My Favorite Drills:

-Pregame: two ball and finishing practice (search Steph Curry pregame)

-Layups: Mikan Drill and floater finishes

-Dribble: Cone Dribble (using 5 dribble moves)

-Shooting: Catch and Shoot from 5 Spots but at game speed

Game Moves: Rip through, jabs, and shot fakes to get shots or layups.

Create Your own Workout (Sample)

Warm Up (5-10 minutes)

-High knees, Butt Kicks, Punter kicks, Balance pulls, Forward lunges with Rotation

Ball Handling (10 minutes)

2 ball dribbling (5 minutes) (stay low, keep head up) Do each drill below for 1 minute Bounce at ankle, bounce at knee, bounce at hip (dribbles bounce at same time) - Bounce at ankle, bounce at knee, bounce at hip (dribbles should **alternate** when they hit the ground) -V dribbles in front of your body -V dribbles on the side of your body -2 dribbles and then cross the ball over **Dribble full court with cones 5 moves (5 minutes)**

Finishing (10 minutes)

Mikan Drill -make 15 layups with both right hand and your left -In and Out (pro hop finish) -Crossover (euro step finish) -Behind the back (floater finish)-Through the legs (jump shot finish)-Spin Move (reverse layup finish)

Shooting (20-30 minutes)
-Stay low, use your legs, and follow through **-make at least 10 shots from the 5 spots** (5 spots are: both corners, elbow area both sides, top of the key) **Bonus:** Make at least 3 pull up jumpers at each spot

Extra (10 minutes) Practice all 3 moves(**find your go to move**) -Rip through to jump stop layup -Rip through, pump fake to euro step layup -Rip through, pump fake, crossover to floater

Create Your own Workout

Warm Up (_____ minutes)

Ball Handling (_____ minutes)

_____

_____

_____

Finishing (_____ minutes)

_____

_____

_____

Shooting (_____ minutes)

_____

_____

_____

Extra (_____ minutes)

_____

_____

_____

Create Your own Workout

Warm Up (_____ minutes)

_____

Ball Handling (_____ minutes)

_____
_____
_____

Finishing (_____ minutes)

_____
_____
_____

Shooting (_____ minutes)

_____
_____
_____

Extra (_____ minutes)

_____
_____
_____

(Sample Journal Entry)
Date: 8/2/2018
I am thankful for:

1.   my coach helping me shoot yesterday
2.   my amazing breakfast this morning

Today my goal is to improve these skills:

My 3 point shot and getting the shot off with a quick release in game like situations.

My workout results today were:

Today I practiced catch and shoot three's from 5 spots on the court, below are my results.
Right Corner : 4-10, Right Wing 6-10, Middle 5-10, Left Wing 7-10, Left Corner 5-10

Today I did best:
Shooting from the wings and left corner.

I can improve on:
Right Corner shooting, tomorrow I will shoot 20 attempts at the spot focusing on my balance.

Date: _____

I am thankful for:

1. _____
2. _____

Today my goal is to improve
these skills:

_____
_____
_____

My workout results today were:

_____
_____
_____
_____

Today I did best:

_____
_____

I can improve on:

_____

Date: _____

I am thankful for:

3. _____

4. _____

Today my goal is to improve
these skills:

_____

_____

_____

My workout results today were:

_____

_____

_____

_____

Today I did best:

_____

_____

I can improve on:

_____

Date: _____

I am thankful for:

1. _____
2. _____

Today my goal is to improve
these skills:

_____
_____
_____

My workout results today were:

_____
_____
_____
_____

Today I did best:

_____
_____

I can improve on:

_____

Date: _____

I am thankful for:

1. _____
2. _____

Today my goal is to improve
these skills:

_____
_____
_____

My workout results today were:

_____
_____
_____
_____

Today I did best:

_____
_____

I can improve on:

_____

Date: _____

I am thankful for:

1. _____
2. _____

Today my goal is to improve
these skills:

_____

_____

_____

My workout results today were:

_____

_____

_____

_____

Today I did best:

_____

_____

I can improve on:

_____

Date: _____

I am thankful for:

1. _____
2. _____

Today my goal is to improve
these skills:

_____

_____

_____

My workout results today were:

_____

_____

_____

_____

Today I did best:

_____

_____

I can improve on:

_____

Date: _____

I am thankful for:

1. _____
2. _____

Today my goal is to improve
these skills:

_____

_____

_____

My workout results today were:

_____

_____

_____

_____

Today I did best:

_____

_____

I can improve on:

_____

Date: _____

I am thankful for:

1. _____
2. _____

Today my goal is to improve
these skills:

_____
_____
_____

My workout results today were:

_____
_____
_____
_____

Today I did best:

_____
_____

I can improve on:

_____

Date: _____

I am thankful for:

1. _____
2. _____

Today my goal is to improve
these skills:

_____
_____
_____

My workout results today were:

_____
_____
_____
_____

Today I did best:

_____
_____

I can improve on:

_____

Date: _____

I am thankful for:

1. _____
2. _____

Today my goal is to improve
these skills:

_____
_____
_____

My workout results today were:

_____
_____
_____
_____

Today I did best:

_____
_____

I can improve on:

_____

Date: _____

I am thankful for:

1. _____

2. _____

Today my goal is to improve
these skills:

_____

_____

_____

My workout results today were:

_____

_____

_____

_____

Today I did best:

_____

_____

I can improve on:

_____

Date: _____

I am thankful for:

1. _____
2. _____

Today my goal is to improve
these skills:

_____

_____

_____

My workout results today were:

_____

_____

_____

_____

Today I did best:

_____

_____

I can improve on:

_____

Date: _____

I am thankful for:

1. _____
2. _____

Today my goal is to improve
these skills:

_____
_____
_____

My workout results today were:

_____
_____
_____
_____

Today I did best:

_____
_____

I can improve on:

_____

Date: _____

I am thankful for:

1. _____
2. _____

Today my goal is to improve
these skills:

_____
_____
_____

My workout results today were:

_____
_____
_____
_____

Today I did best:

_____
_____

I can improve on:

_____

Date: _____

I am thankful for:

1. _____
2. _____

Today my goal is to improve
these skills:

_____
_____
_____

My workout results today were:

_____
_____
_____
_____

Today I did best:

_____
_____

I can improve on:

_____

Date: _____

I am thankful for:

1. _____
2. _____

Today my goal is to improve
these skills:

_____
_____
_____

My workout results today were:

_____
_____
_____
_____

Today I did best:

_____
_____

I can improve on:

_____

Date: _____

I am thankful for:

1. _____
2. _____

Today my goal is to improve
these skills:

_____
_____
_____

My workout results today were:

_____
_____
_____
_____

Today I did best:

_____
_____

I can improve on:

_____

Date: _____

I am thankful for:

1. _____
2. _____

Today my goal is to improve
these skills:

_____

_____

_____

My workout results today were:

_____

_____

_____

_____

Today I did best:

_____

_____

I can improve on:

_____

Date: _____

I am thankful for:

1. _____
2. _____

Today my goal is to improve
these skills:

_____
_____
_____

My workout results today were:

_____
_____
_____
_____

Today I did best:

_____
_____

I can improve on:

_____

Date: _____

I am thankful for:

1. _____
2. _____

Today my goal is to improve
these skills:

_____

_____

_____

My workout results today were:

_____

_____

_____

_____

Today I did best:

_____

_____

I can improve on:

_____

Date: _____

I am thankful for:

1. _____
2. _____

Today my goal is to improve
these skills:

_____
_____
_____

My workout results today were:

_____
_____
_____
_____

Today I did best:

_____
_____

I can improve on:

_____

Date: _____

I am thankful for:

1. _____
2. _____

Today my goal is to improve
these skills:

_____

_____

_____

My workout results today were:

_____

_____

_____

_____

Today I did best:

_____

_____

I can improve on:

_____

Date: _____

I am thankful for:

1. _____
2. _____

Today my goal is to improve
these skills:

_____

_____

_____

My workout results today were:

_____

_____

_____

_____

Today I did best:

_____

_____

I can improve on:

_____

Date: _____

I am thankful for:

1. _____
2. _____

Today my goal is to improve
these skills:

_____
_____
_____

My workout results today were:

_____
_____
_____
_____

Today I did best:

_____
_____

I can improve on:

_____

Date: _____

I am thankful for:

1. _____
2. _____

Today my goal is to improve
these skills:

_____

_____

_____

My workout results today were:

_____

_____

_____

_____

Today I did best:

_____

_____

I can improve on:

_____

Date: _____

I am thankful for:

1. _____
2. _____

Today my goal is to improve
these skills:

_____

_____

_____

My workout results today were:

_____

_____

_____

_____

Today I did best:

_____

_____

I can improve on:

_____

Date: _____

I am thankful for:

1. _____
2. _____

Today my goal is to improve
these skills:

_____

_____

_____

My workout results today were:

_____

_____

_____

_____

Today I did best:

_____

_____

I can improve on:

_____

Date: _____

I am thankful for:

1. _____
2. _____

Today my goal is to improve
these skills:

_____
_____
_____

My workout results today were:

_____
_____
_____
_____

Today I did best:

_____
_____

I can improve on:

_____

Date: _____

I am thankful for:

1. _____
2. _____

Today my goal is to improve
these skills:

_____

_____

_____

My workout results today were:

_____

_____

_____

_____

Today I did best:

_____

_____

I can improve on:

_____

Date: _____

I am thankful for:

1. _____
2. _____

Today my goal is to improve
these skills:

_____
_____
_____

My workout results today were:

_____
_____
_____
_____

Today I did best:

_____
_____

I can improve on:

_____

Date: _____

I am thankful for:

1. _____
2. _____

Today my goal is to improve
these skills:

_____
_____
_____

My workout results today were:

_____
_____
_____
_____

Today I did best:

_____
_____

I can improve on:

_____

Date: _____

I am thankful for:

1. _____
2. _____

Today my goal is to improve
these skills:

_____
_____
_____

My workout results today were:

_____
_____
_____
_____

Today I did best:

_____
_____

I can improve on:

_____

Date: _____

I am thankful for:

1. _____
2. _____

Today my goal is to improve
these skills:

_____
_____
_____

My workout results today were:

_____
_____
_____
_____

Today I did best:

_____
_____

I can improve on:

_____

Date: _____

I am thankful for:

1. _____
2. _____

Today my goal is to improve
these skills:

_____

_____

_____

My workout results today were:

_____

_____

_____

_____

Today I did best:

_____

_____

I can improve on:

_____

Date: _____

I am thankful for:

1. _____
2. _____

Today my goal is to improve
these skills:

_____

_____

_____

My workout results today were:

_____

_____

_____

_____

Today I did best:

_____

_____

I can improve on:

_____

Date: _____

I am thankful for:

1. _____
2. _____

Today my goal is to improve
these skills:

_____
_____
_____

My workout results today were:

_____
_____
_____
_____

Today I did best:

_____
_____

I can improve on:

_____

Date: _____

I am thankful for:

1. _____
2. _____

Today my goal is to improve
these skills:

_____
_____
_____

My workout results today were:

_____
_____
_____
_____

Today I did best:

_____
_____

I can improve on:

_____

Date: _____

I am thankful for:

1. _____
2. _____

Today my goal is to improve
these skills:

_____
_____
_____

My workout results today were:

_____
_____
_____
_____

Today I did best:

_____
_____

I can improve on:

_____

Date: _____

I am thankful for:

1. _____
2. _____

Today my goal is to improve
these skills:

_____

_____

_____

My workout results today were:

_____

_____

_____

_____

Today I did best:

_____

_____

I can improve on:

_____

Date: _____

I am thankful for:

1. _____
2. _____

Today my goal is to improve
these skills:

_____
_____
_____

My workout results today were:

_____
_____
_____
_____

Today I did best:

_____
_____

I can improve on:

_____

Date: _____

I am thankful for:

1. _____
2. _____

Today my goal is to improve
these skills:

_____

_____

_____

My workout results today were:

_____

_____

_____

_____

Today I did best:

_____

_____

I can improve on:

_____

Date: _____

I am thankful for:

1. _____
2. _____

Today my goal is to improve
these skills:

_____
_____
_____

My workout results today were:

_____
_____
_____
_____

Today I did best:

_____
_____

I can improve on:

_____

Date: _____

I am thankful for:

1. _____
2. _____

Today my goal is to improve
these skills:

_____
_____
_____

My workout results today were:

_____
_____
_____
_____

Today I did best:

_____
_____

I can improve on:

_____

Date: _____

I am thankful for:

1. _____
2. _____

Today my goal is to improve
these skills:

_____
_____
_____

My workout results today were:

_____
_____
_____
_____

Today I did best:

_____
_____

I can improve on:

_____

Date: _____

I am thankful for:

1. _____
2. _____

Today my goal is to improve
these skills:

_____

_____

_____

My workout results today were:

_____

_____

_____

_____

Today I did best:

_____

_____

I can improve on:

_____

Date: _____

I am thankful for:

1. _____
2. _____

Today my goal is to improve
these skills:

_____
_____
_____

My workout results today were:

_____
_____
_____
_____

Today I did best:

_____
_____

I can improve on:

_____

Date: _____

I am thankful for:

1. _____
2. _____

Today my goal is to improve
these skills:

_____

_____

_____

My workout results today were:

_____

_____

_____

_____

Today I did best:

_____

_____

I can improve on:

_____

Date: _____

I am thankful for:

1. _____
2. _____

Today my goal is to improve
these skills:

_____
_____
_____

My workout results today were:

_____
_____
_____
_____

Today I did best:

_____
_____

I can improve on:

_____

Date: _____

I am thankful for:

1. _____
2. _____

Today my goal is to improve
these skills:

_____
_____
_____

My workout results today were:

_____
_____
_____
_____

Today I did best:

_____
_____

I can improve on:

_____

Date: _____

I am thankful for:

1. _____
2. _____

Today my goal is to improve
these skills:

_____
_____
_____

My workout results today were:

_____
_____
_____
_____

Today I did best:

_____
_____

I can improve on:

_____

Date: _____

I am thankful for:

1. _____

2. _____

Today my goal is to improve
these skills:

_____

_____

_____

My workout results today were:

_____

_____

_____

_____

Today I did best:

_____

_____

I can improve on:

_____

Date: _____

I am thankful for:

1. _____

2. _____

Today my goal is to improve
these skills:

_____

_____

_____

My workout results today were:

_____

_____

_____

_____

Today I did best:

_____

_____

I can improve on:

_____

Date: _____

I am thankful for:

1. _____
2. _____

Today my goal is to improve
these skills:

_____
_____
_____

My workout results today were:

_____
_____
_____
_____

Today I did best:

_____
_____

I can improve on:

_____

Date: _____

I am thankful for:

1. _____
2. _____

Today my goal is to improve
these skills:

_____
_____
_____

My workout results today were:

_____
_____
_____
_____

Today I did best:

_____
_____

I can improve on:

_____

Date: _____

I am thankful for:

1. _____
2. _____

Today my goal is to improve
these skills:

_____
_____
_____

My workout results today were:

_____
_____
_____
_____

Today I did best:

_____
_____

I can improve on:

_____

Date: _____

I am thankful for:

1. _____
2. _____

Today my goal is to improve
these skills:

_____
_____
_____

My workout results today were:

_____
_____
_____
_____

Today I did best:

_____
_____

I can improve on:

_____

Date: _____

I am thankful for:

1. _____
2. _____

Today my goal is to improve
these skills:

_____
_____
_____

My workout results today were:

_____
_____
_____
_____

Today I did best:

_____
_____

I can improve on:

_____

Date: _____

I am thankful for:

1. _____

2. _____

Today my goal is to improve
these skills:

_____

_____

_____

My workout results today were:

_____

_____

_____

_____

Today I did best:

_____

_____

I can improve on:

_____

Date: _____

I am thankful for:

1. _____
2. _____

Today my goal is to improve
these skills:

_____
_____
_____

My workout results today were:

_____
_____
_____
_____

Today I did best:

_____
_____

I can improve on:

_____

Date: _____

I am thankful for:

1. _____
2. _____

Today my goal is to improve
these skills:

_____

_____

_____

My workout results today were:

_____

_____

_____

_____

Today I did best:

_____

_____

I can improve on:

_____

Date: _____

I am thankful for:

1. _____
2. _____

Today my goal is to improve
these skills:

_____
_____
_____

My workout results today were:

_____
_____
_____
_____

Today I did best:

_____
_____

I can improve on:

_____

Date: _____

I am thankful for:

1. _____
2. _____

Today my goal is to improve
these skills:

_____
_____
_____

My workout results today were:

_____
_____
_____
_____

Today I did best:

_____
_____

I can improve on:

_____

Date: _____

I am thankful for:

1. _____
2. _____

Today my goal is to improve
these skills:

_____
_____
_____

My workout results today were:

_____
_____
_____
_____

Today I did best:

_____
_____

I can improve on:

_____

Date: _____

I am thankful for:

1. _____
2. _____

Today my goal is to improve
these skills:

_____
_____
_____

My workout results today were:

_____
_____
_____
_____

Today I did best:

_____
_____

I can improve on:

_____

Date: _____

I am thankful for:

1. _____
2. _____

Today my goal is to improve
these skills:

_____

_____

_____

My workout results today were:

_____

_____

_____

_____

Today I did best:

_____

_____

I can improve on:

_____

Date: _____

I am thankful for:

1. _____
2. _____

Today my goal is to improve
these skills:

_____

_____

_____

My workout results today were:

_____

_____

_____

_____

Today I did best:

_____

_____

I can improve on:

_____

Date: _____

I am thankful for:

1. _____
2. _____

Today my goal is to improve
these skills:

_____
_____
_____

My workout results today were:

_____
_____
_____
_____

Today I did best:

_____
_____

I can improve on:

_____

Date: _____

I am thankful for:

1. _____
2. _____

Today my goal is to improve
these skills:

_____
_____
_____

My workout results today were:

_____
_____
_____
_____

Today I did best:

_____
_____

I can improve on:

_____

Date: _____

I am thankful for:

1. _____
2. _____

Today my goal is to improve
these skills:

_____
_____
_____

My workout results today were:

_____
_____
_____
_____

Today I did best:

_____
_____

I can improve on:

_____

Date: _____

I am thankful for:

1. _____

2. _____

Today my goal is to improve
these skills:

_____

_____

_____

My workout results today were:

_____

_____

_____

_____

Today I did best:

_____

_____

I can improve on:

_____

Date: _____

I am thankful for:

1. _____
2. _____

Today my goal is to improve
these skills:

_____
_____
_____

My workout results today were:

_____
_____
_____
_____

Today I did best:

_____
_____

I can improve on:

_____

Date: _____

I am thankful for:

1. _____
2. _____

Today my goal is to improve
these skills:

_____
_____
_____

My workout results today were:

_____
_____
_____
_____

Today I did best:

_____
_____

I can improve on:

_____

Date: _____

I am thankful for:

1. _____
2. _____

Today my goal is to improve
these skills:

_____

_____

_____

My workout results today were:

_____

_____

_____

_____

Today I did best:

_____

_____

I can improve on:

_____

Date: _____

I am thankful for:

1. _____
2. _____

Today my goal is to improve
these skills:

_____
_____
_____

My workout results today were:

_____
_____
_____
_____

Today I did best:

_____
_____

I can improve on:

_____

Date: _____

I am thankful for:

1. _____
2. _____

Today my goal is to improve
these skills:

_____
_____
_____

My workout results today were:

_____
_____
_____
_____

Today I did best:

_____
_____

I can improve on:

_____

Date: _____

I am thankful for:

1. _____
2. _____

Today my goal is to improve
these skills:

_____
_____
_____

My workout results today were:

_____
_____
_____
_____

Today I did best:

_____
_____

I can improve on:

_____

Date: _____

I am thankful for:

1. _____
2. _____

Today my goal is to improve
these skills:

_____
_____
_____

My workout results today were:

_____
_____
_____
_____

Today I did best:

_____
_____

I can improve on:

_____

Date: _____

I am thankful for:

1. _____
2. _____

Today my goal is to improve
these skills:

_____
_____
_____

My workout results today were:

_____
_____
_____
_____

Today I did best:

_____
_____

I can improve on:

_____

Date: _____

I am thankful for:

1. _____
2. _____

Today my goal is to improve
these skills:

_____
_____
_____

My workout results today were:

_____
_____
_____
_____

Today I did best:

_____
_____

I can improve on:

_____

Date: _____

I am thankful for:

1. _____
2. _____

Today my goal is to improve
these skills:

_____
_____
_____

My workout results today were:

_____
_____
_____
_____

Today I did best:

_____
_____

I can improve on:

_____

Date: _____

I am thankful for:

1. _____
2. _____

Today my goal is to improve
these skills:

_____
_____
_____

My workout results today were:

_____
_____
_____
_____

Today I did best:

_____
_____

I can improve on:

_____

Date: _____

I am thankful for:

1. _____
2. _____

Today my goal is to improve
these skills:

_____
_____
_____

My workout results today were:

_____
_____
_____
_____

Today I did best:

_____
_____

I can improve on:

_____

Date: _____

I am thankful for:

1. _____
2. _____

Today my goal is to improve
these skills:

_____

_____

_____

My workout results today were:

_____

_____

_____

_____

Today I did best:

_____

_____

I can improve on:

_____

Date: _____

I am thankful for:

1. _____
2. _____

Today my goal is to improve
these skills:

_____
_____
_____

My workout results today were:

_____
_____
_____
_____

Today I did best:

_____
_____

I can improve on:

_____

Date: _____

I am thankful for:

1. _____
2. _____

Today my goal is to improve
these skills:

_____

_____

_____

My workout results today were:

_____

_____

_____

_____

Today I did best:

_____

_____

I can improve on:

_____

Date: _____

I am thankful for:

1. _____
2. _____

Today my goal is to improve
these skills:

_____
_____
_____

My workout results today were:

_____
_____
_____
_____

Today I did best:

_____
_____

I can improve on:

_____

Date: _____

I am thankful for:

1. _____
2. _____

Today my goal is to improve
these skills:

_____

_____

_____

My workout results today were:

_____

_____

_____

_____

Today I did best:

_____

_____

I can improve on:

_____

Date: _____

I am thankful for:

1. _____
2. _____

Today my goal is to improve
these skills:

_____
_____
_____

My workout results today were:

_____
_____
_____
_____

Today I did best:

_____
_____

I can improve on:

_____

Date: _____

I am thankful for:

1. _____
2. _____

Today my goal is to improve
these skills:

_____
_____
_____

My workout results today were:

_____
_____
_____
_____

Today I did best:

_____
_____

I can improve on:

_____

Date: _____

I am thankful for:

1. _____
2. _____

Today my goal is to improve
these skills:

_____

_____

_____

My workout results today were:

_____

_____

_____

_____

Today I did best:

_____

_____

I can improve on:

_____

Date: _____

I am thankful for:

1. _____
2. _____

Today my goal is to improve
these skills:

_____

_____

_____

My workout results today were:

_____

_____

_____

_____

Today I did best:

_____

_____

I can improve on:

_____

Date: _____

I am thankful for:

1. _____
2. _____

Today my goal is to improve
these skills:

_____

_____

_____

My workout results today were:

_____

_____

_____

_____

Today I did best:

_____

_____

I can improve on:

_____

About The Author

My name is Jake Beaman. I grew up loving the game of basketball in the San Francisco, Bay Area. At that time the Warriors were pretty awful but like most classmates we idolized Jordan and Kobe. I was a solid high school player but really learned the game and fell in love with player development when I was a student manager at San Diego State. At SDSU there was an incredible coaching staff under Hall of Fame coach Steve Fisher. Throughout my training career I have had the privilege to work with current NBA coaches and train NBA players. I now work in education with a Masters Degree in Human Rights Education and continue to train all athletes ranging from 5 year olds to current professionals. If you would like to reach me you can find me at jake.beaman33@gmail.com. I hope this journal helps your organize your thoughts and skills to become the best player you can be!

My Basketball Journal

49636175R00074

Made in the USA
Columbia, SC
25 January 2019